Modern computer parts are small but powerful

Computers

Anne Fitzpatrick

A⁺
Smart Apple Media

COPYRIGHT

✎ Published by Smart Apple Media

1980 Lookout Drive, North Mankato, MN 56003

Designed by Rita Marshall

Printed in the United States of America

✎ Photographs by Corbis (Jerry Cooke, Paul Hardy, Peter Johnson), Science Photo Library (George Bernard, J-L Charmet, Andrew Syred), Tom Stack & Associates (TSADO/NASA), Timepix (Ted Thai), Unicorn Stock Photos (Charles E. Schmidt)

✎ Library of Congress Cataloging-in-Publication Data

Fitzpatrick, Anne, 1978– Computers / by Anne Fitzpatrick.

p. cm. – (Great inventions) Includes bibliographical references.

Summary: An introduction to the ideas and technical developments that produced today's computers. Includes a "hands on" activity.

✎ ISBN 1-58340-318-3

1. Computers–History–Juvenile literature. [1. Computers.] I. Title. II. Great inventions (Mankato, Minn.).

QA76.52.F58 2003   004.09–dc21   2002042790

✎ First Edition 9 8 7 6 5 4 3 2 1

Computers

CONTENTS

The word "computer" comes from the word "compute," which means to calculate or work out a math problem. Today, we use computers to write, draw, play games, communicate, and store information. But all of these things still require millions of calculations that take place inside the computer.

About 2,500 years ago, people used stone trays covered with dust or sand to do large calculations. They would make fingerprints in the dust and then count them. Soon people

Long ago, people used rocks to add and subtract

started using pebbles instead of fingerprints. Eventually they

started stringing beads on wires. They had invented the

abacus! With a lot of practice, a person could use the abacus

to add and subtract large numbers quickly. **Blaise Pascal**
invented his
calculator in
But not many people were very fast **order to help**
his father, who
with the abacus. People knew it would be **was a tax**
much better if there were a machine that **collector.**

could do all the work. In 1643, a French mathematician named

Blaise Pascal built a **mechanical** calculator made of wheels

The mechanical calculator was invented in the 1600s

labeled with the numbers 0 through 9. When the first wheel

was turned past 9, it moved the wheel next to it so that

together the two wheels showed the number 10. It had six

wheels, so it could add and subtract numbers up to 999,999.

Electric Brains

Over the next 300 years, Pascal's mechanical

calculator was improved. Adding machines and automatic cash

registers became common by the 1800s. But it was not until

the invention of electricity that machines started to resemble

human brains, able to do all kinds of complicated calculations.

Around 1930, scientists realized that a machine could send and receive signals by turning electricity on and off. A machine that used these electric signals to represent numbers

Adding machines like this were used in the 1800s

could make calculations very quickly. It would not have to wait

for a complicated system of wheels and gears to arrive at an

answer. In 1946, two men named John Mauchly and John

Eckert Jr. built a machine called the **If it had been built in 1950 using transistors, a Game Boy would have filled a large room.**

Electronic Numerical Integrator and

Calculator (ENIAC). Using vacuum

(airless) tubes to control a stream of

electricity, it could calculate 1,000 times faster than a person

with an abacus. ENIAC was made up of more than 18,000

glass tubes and took up 1,500 square feet (139 sq m).

Smaller Is Better

ENIAC was too big to be practical for the average

person. But in 1947, the transistor was invented. Transistors

An entire room was needed for ENIAC and its parts

used **silicon** to carry the electricity. Compared to vacuum tubes, transistors were much smaller, used less electricity, and did not break or wear out as easily. Then, in 1959, scientists learned to make silicon **microchips** that were so small they had to be built under a microscope. ✍ Microchips made computers even smaller, cheaper, and more reliable than transistors had. This made the personal computer (PC), or home computer, possible. The first PC was

A silicon chip is about the size of Lincoln's head on a penny— small enough to be carried by an ant.

This photograph shows just how tiny a microchip is

the Apple II, built in 1978 by Steve Jobs and Steve Wozniak, two friends who were interested in electronics. It came in a plastic case and had a keyboard and a color screen. Soon computers became a common sight in people's homes.

Today and Tomorrow

It is impossible to imagine life without computers today. We use computers to send e-mail, do homework, and play games. There are also many computers all around us. Every time we switch on a light, we are using a computer. Every time we use a camera, microwave, or car, we are using a computer.

Even objects that do not have computers inside them, such as

food or clothing, were probably made with the help of com-

puters. ✍ Computers will continue to become more and

Laptop computers are light and fold up like a book

more important in our lives. Someday, our houses will probably have computers to turn lights, heat, and air conditioning on and off automatically. Computers may cook, clean, and keep watch for fires and burglars. We might even carry tiny computers in our bodies to keep watch for illness. The possibilities are endless. What else might computers do for you?

Powerful "supercomputers" are used for complicated tasks such as designing rockets and predicting weather.

Scientists use computers to help launch space shuttles

The Great Race

The computer was invented because people wanted a faster way to do calculations. Try this activity to find out if they succeeded.

What You Need

10 pennies, 10 nickels, 10 dimes, and 10 quarters
A calculator   A computer   Two friends

What You Do

1. Make an abacus by using the pennies to count by ones, the nickels to count by fives, the dimes to count by tens, and the quarters to count by hundreds.
2. One person will use the coin "abacus," another will use the calculator, and the third person will use the calculator program on a computer.
3. Find the answers to the following math problems using the abacus, the calculator, and the computer, starting at the same time.

$$247 + 186 \qquad 446 - 189 \qquad 62 \times 11$$

Who finishes the problems first? Who finishes second? Does everyone have the right answers?

Coins can be used in a simple counting system

INFORMATION

Index

Words to Know

abacus (AB-uh-kus)—a frame with rods or wires on which beads are moved to do arithmetic calculations

mechanical (meh-KAN-ih-kul)—put into action by physical power such as wheels and levers

microchips (MY-crow-chips)—tiny pieces of silicon engraved with lines that carry and control electricity

silicon (SIH-lih-kon)—a hard, dark gray, nonmetallic substance found in most rocks

transistors (tran-ZIS-turz)—small devices made of metal, silicon, and wires that carry and control electricity

Read More

Doherty, Gillian. *101 Things to Do With Your Computer*. Tulsa, Okla.: EDC Publishing, 1998.

Kalman, Bobbie. *The Computer from A to Z*. New York: Crabtree Publishers, 1998.

Internet Sites

BrainPOP: Computer and Digital Technology
http://www.brainpop.com/tech/computeranddigital/

Click-N-Learn What's Inside A Computer
http://www.kidsonline.net/learn/c_n_l.html

The Ultimate Computer Source
http://library.thinkquest.org/25018/